C000064918

Death and Burial Records for Family Historians

Stuart A. Raymond

VITAL.
RECORDS
FOR FAMILY
HISTORIANS
3

THE FAMILY HISTORY PARTNERSHIP

Published by
The Family History Partnership
57 Bury New Road, Ramsbottom
Bury, Lancashire BL0 0BZ
Webpage: **www.familyhistorypartnership.co.uk**
Email: sales@thefamilyhistorypartnership.com

in association with
S.A. & M.J. Raymond
38 Princess Gardens
Trowbridge, Wiltshire BA14 7PT

Webpage: **www.stuartraymond.co.uk**
Email: samjraymond@btopenworld.com

ISBN: 978 1 906280 26 0

© S.A. & M.J. Raymond

First Published 2011

Cover illustration:
Cholera Burial in Southernhay, Exeter, from
SHAPTER, THOMAS, *The history of cholera in Exeter in 1832*,
John Churchill, 1849.

Printed and bound by
Information Press. Southfield Road, Eynsham
Oxford OX29 4JB

Contents

Acknowledgements

I would like to thank the members of the Family History Partnership for their support, and especially Richard Ratcliffe, who read my manuscript, and Bob Boyd, who saw the book through the press.

1. Introduction

Death, sadly, is a part of the human condition. All of our ancestors have died, and most have been buried. Fortunately for family historians, most UK deaths and/or burials in the last two or three centuries have been recorded. There are many records which go back further than that. The records of deaths and burials are capable of yielding much information about our ancestors, and may be very useful for tracing pedigrees. This book identifies the available records, where to find them, the information they contain, and how to use them.

Civil registers of deaths have been compiled in England and Wales since 1837. Burials have been recorded in parish registers since 1538. Most registers from the eighteenth century and later have survived. Many earlier registers are also available, although others have been lost through the ravages of war, fire, flood, mice, and all the other enemies of paper and parchment records.

A wide range of other records are also available. Cemetery registers have been kept since the late nineteenth century. Many nonconformists and other denominations have maintained their own burial registers. Churchyards and cemeteries are full of monumental inscriptions, which sometimes contain masses of family history information. Wills, newspaper obituaries, and funeral certificates, were compiled either immediately before, or immediately after, death. Other records took longer to prepare, but resulted from death. Landlords used their manorial court rolls to record their tenants' deaths, and the names of heirs; inquisitions post mortem recorded similar information for the Crown's tenants in chief. A variety of other death and burial records may be found.

The information provided by these sources varies. All normally give dates of death and/or burial. Some give ages or places of birth, which may enable you to trace earlier generations. Others may give details of the deceased's tenancies, or list some of his relatives, both of which may be useful for tracing his family. Some sources may give much more information; monumental inscriptions, for example, frequently list several generations of the same family. Records of deaths and burials are invaluable sources for tracing our ancestors, and for throwing light on their lives.

Burials in the London area can be particularly difficult to trace. The civil registers do not indicate places of burial. Parish and cemetery registers are deposited in a large number of different repositories. A variety of different burial indexes are available, but there is no single centralized index. For a useful overview of the problem, and some solutions, consult:

- A Guide to Burials in the London Area
  www.rootschat.com/forum/index.php/board,24.0.html
  (Click title)

2. Civil Registers

All deaths which have occurred in England and Wales since 1st July 1837 should be recorded in the civil registers of deaths. The easiest way to obtain information about an individual's death is therefore to obtain a death certificate from the General Register Office (GRO), or from the relevant district registrar.

Death certificates provide the following information:
1. When and where died
2. Name and surname
3. Sex
4. Age (from June 1866)
5. Occupation
6. Cause of death
7. Name (signature), description and residence of informant
8. When registered
9. Signature of registrar

Since 1969, additional information has been provided. This includes the date of birth, the birthplace, and, for married women and widows, their maiden names. When registration began in 1837, the onus for registering deaths was placed on registrars, although burial could only take place after the registrar had certified to the undertaker that the death had been registered. The Births and Deaths Registration Act of 1874 placed the onus for reporting deaths onto relatives who were present. This Act also required registered medical practitioners to certify the cause of death. If this could not be done, the death had to be reported to a coroner, who could, if he thought it necessary, order a post mortem examination.

Death certificates can be obtained from the GRO, or from the registrar of the district where the death took place. Both require the consultation of indexes. The indexes of the GRO, and those of district registrars, are quite distinct from each other, and cannot be used interchangeably. The GRO, for a fee, will consult its indexes for you. They are, however, publicly available on the internet, and on microfilm/fiche in various libraries and record offices.

Free searches of most GRO death indexes prior to the mid-1940s can be made at:
- FreeBMD
  www.freebmd.org.uk

More extensive indexes are available on a number of commercial internet sites. These may charge a fee for searching. Currently, they include:
- 192.com
  www.192.com/people

- Ancestry
  www.ancestry.co.uk
- BMD Index
  www.bmdindex.co.uk
- Family Relatives
  www.familyrelatives.com
- Find My Past
  www.findmypast.co.uk

For libraries and record offices which hold the indexes, consult:
- Public Holders of the GRO indexes
  **www.direct.gov.uk/prod_consum_dg/groups/dg_digitalassets/@dg/
  @en/@government/documents/digitalasset/dg_184626.pdf**

The GRO indexes were compiled quarterly until 1984. Since then, they have been compiled annually. It may be necessary to consult the index for more than one quarter. A death which took place at the end of one quarter may well be registered in the following quarter.

Against the name of each individual, the index gives the registration district where the death was registered, the volume number of the register, and the page number. These are the details needed to order certificates from the GRO. They can be ordered online or by phone. For details of the procedure to be followed, visit:
- Order Birth, Marriage and Death Certificates
  **www.direct.gov.uk/en/Governmentcitizensandrights/Registeringlifeevents/
  Birthmarriageanddeathcertificates/DG_175628**

Certificates can also be obtained from the registrar of the district where the death was registered. The procedure for doing so varies between registrars. District registrars have compiled their own indexes (which cannot be used to order certificates from the GRO). In some instances these can be viewed by researchers; elsewhere they must be searched by the staff of the Registrar. Registrars are listed in:
- LANGSTON, BRETT. *A handbook to the registration districts of England and Wales*. B. Langston, 2001.
- Registration Districts in England & Wales (1837-1974)
  www.ukbmd.org.uk/genuki/REG/index.htm

An increasing number of indexes to the registers held by district registrars are available on the internet. These are generally free, and can be identified by consulting:
- UK BMD: Local BMD: Sites with indexes based on original Register Office Records
  http//ukcensus.org.uk/local_bmd

Various problems may occur when searching indexes to death registers. It is important to appreciate the bureaucratic procedures used by registrars. Registers were compiled for each registration district, where they are still retained. District Registrars copied the entries in these in order to make a quarterly return to the GRO. GRO clerks copied these returns into their own registers, and then compiled an index. There were consequently no less than four opportunities for mistakes to occur. And occur they did. The GRO's indexes are so inaccurate that it has proved necessary to compile an entirely new index. This project is currently in progress, and may take several years to complete. There will no doubt be an announcement on the Identity and Passport Service website **www.homeoffice. gov.uk/agencies-public-bodies/ips** (the GRO is part of this Service) when the new index becomes available.

Some information from the GRO's register will be unavailable until the new index is completed. However, many elusive entries can be tracked down by researchers. Points that need to be borne in mind include the following:

- Name spellings vary. It is a myth that they never change. If an initial search fails, try searching alternative spellings. For example, Smith could by Smythe, Hockey could be Hokey, Bennett could be Benet. Forenames may also differ. Smith, Robert, may be a long way from Smith, Bob in the index, yet it is the same name. For a useful guide to first name variants, consult Alan Bardsley's *First name variants* (3rd ed. FFHS, 2003).
- The name given on a death certificate is the name by which the deceased was known at the date of death. It is not necessarily the name used on the birth certificate, or at baptism. Many people changed their names during their lives, not only married women. Such changes were not necessarily recorded officially.
- Deaths could occur anywhere, not necessarily in the deceased's home area. They are recorded in the registration district where the death took place, which is not necessarily where burial took place. If the deceased was travelling or working away from home at the time of his death, registration might take place in a totally unexpected registration district.
- The information provided by death certificates is not necessarily accurate. It may constitute a best guess by someone who did not know the deceased very well, for example, the master of a workhouse or other institution. The information provided by such people must be viewed with caution. Ages in particular may be very dubious. Even the deceased may not have known his or her own exact age.

3. Parish Registers

Prior to the nineteenth century, the vast majority of burials took place in church-yards and churches, and were recorded in parish registers. Nonconformists, who may have preferred to go elsewhere for their baptisms and marriages, frequently insisted on their right to a churchyard burial. Only Quakers and Jews were unlikely to be buried in a churchyard (although a few other nonconformists did have their own burial grounds). Burial entries in parish registers are much more comprehensive than baptism and marriage entries.

Parish registers of baptisms, marriages and burials have been maintained by Anglican clergy since 1538. Where churchyards are still in use, burial registers continue to be maintained today.

In early registers, baptism, marriage and burial entries were frequently entered together, chronologically. This practice ceased after 1753, when Hardwicke's Marriage Act required marriage entries to be made on a printed form - although sometimes baptism and burial entries continued to be made together, at least until 1813, when printed forms were introduced for both events.

The information given in early burial records can be very sparse, although there was originally no standard format. Many registers simply give names and dates. Others may be more informative. Occupations, places of residence, ages, and causes of death are sometimes noted. Sometimes visitations of plague and other diseases prompted more detailed comment; for example, in the register of St. Giles, Durham, is the following entry: '1604. Ann Ourd, wyffe of Christopher Ourd, bur. 25 Jan. So the hole household dyed in the vicitacion at this time, and so ye plague ceased'.

When young children were buried, their parents' names might be recorded. Acts of 1666 and 1678 required bodies to be buried in a woollen shroud, and burial entries frequently record that this had been done. An affidavit had to be made to confirm that the law had been complied with. Sometimes these survive in separate books, and may give useful additional information. This law was repealed in 1814, although by then it had been ignored for many years. Burial entries sometimes also record the duties levied on them between 1694 and 1705, and between 1783 and 1794. Entries marked 'P' or 'EP' in the latter period indicate that the deceased was an 'exempt pauper'.

More informative burial entries were encouraged by Archbishop Markham of York. In 1777, he ordered his clergy to use the format of entry pioneered by William Dade. Dade registers are frequently found in the Dioceses of York and Chester, and sometimes further afield. They give the deceased's name, descent, profession, and abode. The researcher who finds his ancestor's burial in a Dade register will be given many clues to further research.

It was not until 1813 that a standard national format for burial entries in parish registers was adopted. In that year, printed forms modelled on the printed marriage registers used since 1753 were introduced. They required the deceased's name, abode and age to be recorded. The date of burial was also to be entered, together with the name of the clergyman who officiated at the funeral. Unfortunately, occupations were not required, nor any information on the deceased's family.

Parish registers can normally be found in local record offices, unless they are still in use. For a summary listing of English and Welsh registers, consult:
- HUMPHERY-SMITH, CECIL R. *Phillimore atlas and index of parish registers.* 3rd ed. Phillimore, 2002.

More detailed listings, including details of bishops transcripts, modern copies, and indexes, etc., can be found in the authoritative county volumes of the *National index of parish registers*, published by the Society of Genealogists. It may be worth consulting the parish pages of Genuki **www.genuki.org.uk**, and the Family Search Research Wiki **https://wiki.familysearch.org** for up to date information on transcripts, indexes, and new web pages.

Many record offices have placed lists of the parish registers they hold on their websites; these are listed at
- ARCHON Directory
  www.nationalarchives.gov.uk/archon

Record offices have also frequently listed their parish register holdings on:
- A2A: Access to Archives
  www.nationalarchives.gov.uk/a2a

Numerous registers have been transcribed and published. Societies solely devoted to this task exist, or have existed, in a number of counties. Family history societies and county record societies have also published many registers. Others have been privately published by their editors. Most published registers can be identified by consulting:
- Bibliography of British History
  www.history.ac.uk/partners/bbih
  (free searches may be available through the websites of a number of public and university libraries)

Full listings of published registers are given in the county volumes of my *British genealogical library guides* series (formerly *British genealogical bibliographies*).

There are many transcripts and indexes of parish registers on the internet. These are listed in:
- RAYMOND, STUART A. *Births marriages & deaths on the web.* 2 vols. 2nd ed. FFHS, 2005. New edition forthcoming from the Family History Partnership.

Numerous unpublished transcripts can be found in record offices and libraries. A large collection is held by the Society of Genealogists **www.sog.org.uk**. Transcribers have frequently produced three copies, one for this Society, one for their local family history society, and one for the relevant record office or local studies library.

Many parish registers have been microfilmed by the Latter Day Saints (LDS) for their Family History Library. Some of these microfilms are taken directly from original registers; others are transcripts. The International Genealogical Index (IGI) indexes the baptisms and marriages found on these microfilms, but, sadly, not the burial entries. Nevertheless, the registers they have filmed frequently do contain burial entries. They are listed in the Library's catalogue, which can be searched at:

- Family Search
  www.familysearch.org
  (click 'Catalog')

These microfilm can be obtained through the world-wide network of Family Search Centers. There is likely to be one of these near you. Addresses are given on the web-site.

Microfilm or microfiche copies of parish registers can also sometimes be purchased directly from record offices. If your local record office offers this service, details are likely to be given on its websites.

If you consult a microfilm in a Family Search Center, check whether it is taken from the original register or from a transcript. Transcripts can be very useful. They should not, however, be treated as a substitute for original registers. Transcribers are liable to make mistakes. It is always desirable to check the accuracy of transcripts against original registers. Microfilmed original registers are more trustworthy than transcripts, although even they may occasionally miss a frame, or prove indecipherable due to the poor quality of the original register.

It is also important to note that the terms 'transcripts' and 'indexes' are not synonyms - a point that web-masters frequently ignore. A transcript should be an exact copy of the original register. An index is merely an alphabetical list telling you where the entry in the register can be found; it does not necessarily provide all the information to be found in the original docuement. The fact that a burial entry cannot be found in an index does not mean that it is not in the original register.

Digitised images of parish registers are beginning to appear on the internet. At the time of writing only a handful of English collections are available (for Scotland, see below, p.37-8). These include:

- Medway City Ark
  http://cityark.medway.gov.uk
  (click 'parish registers online')
- London Parish Records from 1538
  http://landing.ancestry.co.uk/lma
- Cheshire Parish Register Project
  www.csc.liv.ac.uk/~cprdb

Many more registers are currently being digitised. For example, registers from Manchester, Plymouth and West Devon, and Wales may be available on the internet by 2012. News of these and other projects can be found at http://growyourownfamilytree.wordpress.com. It is probable that many more registers will be digitised in the next few years, as this is the most important genealogical source not currently available in digitised format.

A variety of indexes to the burial entries in parish registers are available. The most important is the National Burial Index (NBI). This is a cooperative project involving many family history societies throughout England and Wales. There are a number of ways in which it can be accessed. The entire NBI is available on CD. The 3rd edition of this CD was published by the Federation of Family History Societies in 2010, and includes 18,400,000 records, from 9,100 burial locations in 50 counties. Full details can be viewed at:
- National Burial Index
  www.ffhs.org.uk/projects/nbi/

Most (but not all) of the NBI can be searched online, together with a number of other databases, at:
- Search Births, Marriages and Deaths 1538 – 2006
  www.findmypast.co.uk/BirthsMarriagesDeaths.jsp

For specific details of the NBI on the Find My Past site, including details of coverage, visit:
- Find My Past: National Burial Index Records
  www.findmypast.co.uk/content/ffhs/nbi.jsp

Each contributing society is willing to search their own portion for researchers. However, not all family history societies have contributed to the NBI. Some, such as the society for Devon **www.devonfhs.org.uk/indexes.htm# Burials,** have their own separate burial indexes. Details of society indexes (whether included in the NBI or not) and search services can normally be found on their web pages, which are listed at:
- Family History and Genealogy Societies
  www.genuki.org.uk/Societies

Another substantial burial index, containing some 36,000 entries, is hosted by British Origins:
- City of London Burials 1781-1904
  www.origins.net/help/aboutbo-clb.aspx

A variety of other indexes (also covering sources such as monumental inscriptions and newspaper obituaries) are listed by:
- GIBSON, JEREMY, & HAMPSON, ELIZABETH. *Specialist indexes for family historians.* 2nd ed. Federation of Family History Societies, 2000.

Further Reading

For an up to date guide to parish registers, consult:

- RAYMOND, STUART A. *Parish registers: a history and guide.* Family History Partnership, 2009.

The classic, but now somewhat dated account, is:

- STEEL, D.J. *National index of parish registers volume 1. Sources of births, marriages and deaths before 1837 (1).* Society of Genealogists, 1968.

4. Bishops' Transcripts

Bishops' transcripts (sometimes referred to as BTs) are copies of parish registers, made annually, and deposited in diocesan registries. A few survive from the sixteenth century; they continued to be made until the nineteenth century. BTs can now be found in local record offices. They have not survived as well as parish registers, but where the latter have been lost they may be the only record of particular vital events. If parish registers and BTs both survive, it is worth comparing them. BTs sometimes provide additional information.

The county volumes of the *National index of parish registers,* which have already been mentioned, will tell you what survives for particular parishes. For an over view, consult:

- GIBSON, JEREMY. *Bishops' transcripts and marriage licences ...* 4th ed. Federation of Family History Societies, 1997. New edition forthcoming from the Family History Partnership.

5. Non-Parochial Registers

Not all Church of England burial services took place in parish churches. There are also a variety of non-parochial burial grounds. Cathedrals, for example, are non-parochial, but numerous burials take place in their precincts. For many centuries, most burials in Exeter took place in the Cathedral Close. Burial grounds may also be found associated with prisons, hospitals, schools, and a variety of other institutions. Details of their registers can be ascertained from the county volumes of the National index of parish registers.

The term 'non-parochial register' is sometimes used to refer to registers kept by nonconconformists. It is better to reserve the term for institutional registers kept by Anglican clergy, although it should be noted that some non-parochial registers are kept with nonconformist registers in the National Archives (TNA). These include, for example:

- Registers of the Rolls Chapel, Chancery Lane (PRO 30/21/3/1). Includes a few burials, 1738-1826.
- Register of the Dockyard Church, Sheerness (ADM 6/431). Includes burials 1807-26
- Greenwich Hospital burial registers, 1844-1981 (ADM 73)

- Chelsea Royal Hospital burial registers, 1705-1864 (RG 4/1669-1676, & RG 8/16-18)
- Foundling Hospital burial register 1741-58 (RG 4/4396)
- Millbank Penitentiary burial register 1848-63 (PCOM 2/165)
- Westminster Penitentiary burial register 1817-53 (PCOM 2/140)

The registers in RG classes noted above are available online at BMD Registers **www.bmdregisters.co.uk**.

6. Cemetery Registers

By the early nineteenth century, churchyards in London and other major cities were becoming increasingly full. In some cases, they had become health hazards. New arrangements for burials were urgently needed. Nonconformists took the lead by establishing Bunhill Fields cemetery in the mid-eighteenth century. In the early nineteenth century, private cemetery companies began to be formed. Burial boards were established in the 1850s to provide public cemeteries. Many large cemeteries were established outside of ecclesiastical jurisdiction. The registers of these cemeteries may still be held by them, or they may have been deposited in local record offices. A few held by TNA are available online at BMD Registers www.bmdregisters.co.uk. These include:

- Bunhill Fields Burial Ground, City Road, 1713-1854 (RG4/3974-4001, 4288-91, & 4633)
- Bunhill Burial Ground, or Golden Lane Cemetery, 1833-53 (RG6/35-8)
- South London Burial Ground, East Street, Walworth, London, 1819-c 1837 (RG4/4362)
- Necropolis Burial Ground, Everton, Liverpool, Merseyside, c 1825-c 1837 (RG4/3121)
- Southwark New Burial Ground, 1821-54 (RG8/73-4)
- Spa Fields, Clerkenwell, 1778-1849 (RG4/4316-22 & 4366-7)
- Victoria Park Cemetery, London, 1853-76 (RG8/42-51)
- Bethnal Green Protestant Dissenters Burying Ground 1793-1837 (RG8/305-14)

A centralised database for UK cemetery registers is currently being developed. At the time of writing, over 1,000,000 entries from 7 burial authorities can be searched, but another 2,000,000 records from 13 authorities are due to be added, with millions more in the pipeline. Visit:
- Deceased Online
  www.deceasedonline.co.uk

Many cemeteries have their own webpages. In a few cases, they also have databases of their registers. The latter are listed in Raymond's *Births marriages and deaths on the web* (see above, p. 9).

For an online international gateway to cemetery webpages (including a few UK sites), visit:
- Interment.net: Cemetery Records Online
  www.interment.net

Cemeteries in Greater London, together with their addresses and details of registers, are listed in:
- WOLFSON, PATRICIA S. *Greater London cemeteries and crematoria*. 7th ed., revised by Cliff Webb. Society of Genealogists Enterprises, 2005.

A comprehensive directory of cemeteries, listing addresses and web pages, but excluding information about registers, can be consulted at:
- The Institute of Cemetery and Crematorium Management's Bereavement Services Portal
  www.iccm-uk.com

Cemetery registers are likely to include names, dates of death, dates of burial or cremation, and perhaps ages, addresses, and occupations. There may also be a burial plot number, or a separate graves book, listing the bodies in each grave. Where these exist, they will enable you to locate your ancestors' actual graves, and perhaps their memorials (see below, pp.21-2). If a family has purchased a burial plot, its deeds may list the bodies resting in a grave.

It may also be possible to find information amongst the records of undertakers. For example, the records of Spicers Undertakers, held by London Metropolitan Archives, provide a considerable amount of information concerning funerals, 1891-1969. You may find, for example, names, addresses, ages, the places of death, where buried or cremated (including plot numbers), and even the sizes of coffins and the costs of the funerals. Similar records have frequently been deposited in local record offices, and many can be found by searching:
- A2A: Access to Archives
  www.nationalarchives.gov.uk/a2a

7. Nonconformist Registers

The term 'nonconformist' is usually used to denote those protestant Christians who refused to conform to the usages and doctrines of the Church of England, and who established their own denominations. The term was first used to refer to Presbyterians, Congregationalists (or Independants), and Baptists, who separated from the Church of England after the Restoration in 1662. It also encompassed Quakers, whose records are considered separately below. Various Methodist denominations were formed in the late eighteenth and nineteenth centuries. In the nineteenth and twentieth centuries a wide variety of denominations and sects have been established, for example, the Salvation Army, Pentecostalists, the Free Church of England, the Church of Jesus Christ of Latter Day Saints.

The great majority of nonconformists prior to the nineteenth century continued to claim their right to burial in parish churchyards. A few congregations, however, established their own burial grounds, and kept their own registers. Most of these are now in TNA, and (together with some non-parochial registers) are available online at:
- BMD Registers
  www.bmdregisters.co.uk

For a full list of the registers in classes RG4 and RG8, which are digitised on this site, see:
- *General Register Office: Registers of births, marriages and deaths surrendered to the Non-parochial Registers Commissions, RG4 & RG8.* 2 vols. List and Index Society, **265-6**. 1996.

Details of nonconformist burial registers can also be found in the county volumes of the *National index of parish registers,* and in a number of volumes of the Society of Genealogists *My ancestors were ...* series. The latter include:
- BREED, GEOFFREY. *My ancestors were Baptists: how can I find out more about them?* 4th ed. Society of Genealogists Enterprises, 2007.
- CLIFFORD, DAVID J.H. *My ancestors were Congregationalists in England and Wales: how can I find out more about them?* 2nd ed. Society of Genealogists, 1997.
- LEARY, WILLIAM. *My ancestors were Methodists: how can I find out more about them?* 4th ed. Society of Genealogists Enterprises, 2005.
- RUSTON, ALAN. *My ancestors were English Presbyterians or Unitarians: how can I find out more about them?* 2nd ed. Society of Genealogists Enterprises, 2001.

Further Reading
- STEEL, D.J. *Sources for nonconformist genealogy and family history.* National index of parish registers 2. Society of Genealogists, 1973.

8. Quaker (or Friends') Registers
Some of the most reliable nonconformist death registers were compiled by the Society of Friends, otherwise known as Quakers. These need to be considered separately. The London Yearly Meeting kept strict control over the activities of other Meetings, and ensured that their records were well kept.

Unlike other nonconformist denominations, most Quakers had their own burial grounds, although some preferred to be buried in their own orchards and fields. Quakers had little reverence for burial places. The family historian seeking a memorial to a Quaker is likely to be disappointed, since until the mid-nineteenth century such things were considered to be vain.

In 1776, Quaker registration procedures were reformed. Quakers were the first to use printed books to record deaths. Their register entries include the name of the deceased, the date of death, age, residence, occupation, and the place of burial. Registration procedures required the preparation of duplicate burial notes by Preparative Meetings. One was sent to the grave-digger, who returned it when he had completed his work in order for the burial to be registered. The duplicate note was sent to the Quarterly Meeting, who also kept a register. Burial notes sometimes survive amongst Meeting archives. Some Meetings also supplemented their death register with a record of wills in which Quakers were named as executors.

A distinguishing feature of Quaker registers is the use of their own dating system. The usual (pagan) names of months and years are not used. Instead, reference is made to the 'sixth month' or the 'second day'.

Quaker registers were surrendered to the Registrar General in 1840-41. More came in in 1857. The surrendered registers are now in TNA, class RG 6. A full listing of them is available:

* *General Register Office. Society of Friends registers, notes, and certificates of births, marriages and deaths.* List & Index Society **267**. 1996. This volume has a useful introduction to the registers. It supersedes previous listings, which should not now be used.

These registers have been digitised, and are now available online at:
* BMD Registers
  www.bmdregisters.co.uk

Before the registers were surrendered, 'digests' were made of them in duplicate, so that the Society could retain the information in them. One copy was retained locally, and is likely to have been deposited in a local record office; the other is now in Friends House Library **www.quaker.org.uk/library**. The Library's copy has been filmed, and the microfilm collection is now available in a number of research libraries:
* *Friends House Library digest registers of births, marriages and burials for England and Wales, 17th c. - 1837.* 32 microfilm reels. World Microfilm Publications, 1989.

After the introduction of civil registration in 1837, Quakers ceased to maintain their death registers. They did, however, retain their burial notice system.

Further Reading
* MILLIGAN, EDWARD H., & THOMAS, MALCOLM J. *My ancestors were Quakers: how can I find out more about them?* 2nd ed. Society of Genealogists, 1999.

9. Huguenot Registers

Many French protestants fled to England to escape persecution in the sixteenth and seventeenth centuries. They established their own churches in England, and kept registers of baptisms and marriages. A few also kept burial registers. However, many Huguenots were buried in Anglican churchyards, and their burials were recorded in parish registers. All surviving Huguenot registers can be searched at BMDRegisters **www.bmdregisters.co.uk**. They have also been published by:

* The Huguenot Society of Great Britain and Ireland
  www.huguenotsociety.org.uk

For details of which Huguenot registers contain burials, consult:
* MULLINS, E.L.C. *Texts and calendars: an analytical guide to serial publications.* Royal Historical Society guides and handbooks **7**. 1958. Supplement 1983.

Further Reading
* CURRER-BRIGGS, N., & GAMBIER, R. *Huguenot ancestry.* Phillimore, 1985.

10. Roman Catholic Registers

In the sixteenth and seventeenth centuries, most Roman Catholics were buried in parish churchyards, sometimes clandestinely. Their burials were recorded in parish registers. Occasionally, burial was refused, and bodies had to be buried in unconsecrated ground. Such burials may also be recorded in parish registers.

After 1800, it became common for Roman Catholic chapels to have their own burial grounds. It was not, however, until the Burial Act of 1852 that they were legalised. A handful of Roman Catholic registers were deposited with the Registrar General in 1840, and are now in TNA, class RG 4. These are available online at BMD Registers **www.bmdregisters.co.uk**. Most registers, however, were retained by the clergy at that time. They have since frequently been deposited in local record offices, and are listed in the county volumes of the *National index of parish registers*. For a full listing, consult:
* GANDY, M. *Catholic missions and registers.* 6 vols. + atlas vol. Michael Gandy, 1993.

Many Roman Catholic registers have been published by the Catholic Record Society. For details, consult:
* Catholic Record Society: Records Series
  www.catholic-history.org.uk/crs/records.htm

Further Reading
* STEEL, D.J., & SAMUEL, EDGAR R. *Sources for Roman Catholic and Jewish genealogy and family history.* National index of parish registers **3**. Phillimore for the Society of Genealogists, 1974.

11. Jewish Registers

Jewish synagogues and cemeteries kept burial registers. A few have been deposited in local record offices (and can sometimes be located on A2A www.nationalarchives.gov.uk/a2a), but many are still held by the Jewish authorities. Records from 23 English cemeteries are indexed in:

- Jewish Gen Online Worldwide Burial Registry
  www.jewishgen.org/databases/Cemetery

Many death announcements and obituaries from leading Jewish newspaper are reprinted in:

- BERGER, DOREEN. *The Jewish Victorian: Genealogical information from the Jewish newspapers, 1861-1870*. Robert Boyd Publications, 2004. A further volume covers 1871-80.

Death announcements from the late nineteenth-century *Jewish Chronicle* are indexed in a series of databases that can be found at:

- Anglo-Jewish Miscellanies
  www.jeffreymaynard.com

For a directory to sources of Jewish burial information, together with a gateway to other sites, visit:

- International Jewish Cemetery Project: British Isles
  www.iajgsjewishcemeteryproject.org//british-isles/index.html

Further Reading

- JOSEPH, ANTHONY. *My ancestors were Jewish*. 4th ed. Society of Genealogists Enterprieses, 2008.
- STEEL, D.J., & SAMUEL, EDGAR R. *Sources for Roman Catholic and Jewish genealogy and family history*. National index of parish registers 3. Phillimore for the Society of Genealogists, 1974.

12. Overseas Registers

Deaths and burials which took place at sea, or in foreign countries, are recorded in a wide variety of different registers, and must be sought in many different record offices. Many overseas events would have been recorded in the registers of foreign jurisdictions, and must be sought in the countries where they took place. These are beyond the scope of this book, although it may be pointed out that much information on overseas registration is available on the internet. A gateway to relevant sites is provided at:

- Cyndis List: Death Records
  www.cyndislist.com/death

Much advice on overseas registers can be found on the LDS website, Family Search **www.familysearch.org/eng** (click 'research helps' and 'guidance'). This site also lists microfilms of many overseas registers (click 'Library'), which can be borrowed through the Family History Library's international network of Family History Centres. Some copies of overseas registers are also held by the Society of Genealogists **www.sog.org**.

The British have devoted a great deal of effort to recording deaths and burials at sea and overseas. Overseas Anglican churches maintained registers, which they sent to the Bishop of London. Consulates maintained registers which they sent to the Foreign Office, who reported deaths to the GRO. Armed forces units overseas also kept registers of the deaths of servicemen and their dependants. British captains reported deaths at sea to the Registrar General of Shipping and Seamen, who passed the information on to the GRO.

The registers returned to the Bishop of London have been deposited in the Guildhall Library, apart from a few in TNA class RG 33 (see p. 20). They include not only original registers, but also some bishops' transcripts, and other copies. There is also a series of 'International Memoranda', 1816 to 1924, which include some burials, although they mainly relate to births/baptisms and marriages. For details of this collection, together with some useful notes on registers held overseas, consult:
* Births, Marriages & Deaths Overseas
  www.history.ac.uk/gh/overseas.htm

A few overseas Anglican registers are also held by Lambeth Palace Library. See:
* Lambeth Palace Library Research Guide: Sources for Family History and Genealogy
  www.lambethpalacelibrary.org/files/Family_History.pdf

From 1854, ships captains had responsibility for making returns of deaths which took place on board their vessels. These were sent to the Registrar General of Shipping and Seamen (RGSS), who compiled registers which are now in TNA:
* BT 158 1854-1890
* BT 159 1875-1888
* BT 334 1891-1972

Classes BT 158-9 have been digitised for BMD Registers **www.bmdregisters. co.uk**. Some of these registers are also available at Find My Past **www. findmypast.com**, although their website does not make it clear which ones.

Deaths registered by the RGSS should have been reported to the GRO, or, where appropriate, to its Scottish and Irish counterparts. It is not clear that this always happened. If it did, then certificates can be obtained as outlined above, p. 5-7 (or p. 32-3 and p. 36-7 for records from Ireland and Scotland). However, if possible, it is better to consult the original RGSS registers, which are likely to be more accurate than those compiled by the GRO.

TNA also holds monthly lists of deaths of seamen for 1886-9 (BT 156), and registers of seamen's deaths classified by causes for 1882-8 (BT 157). Registers of the wages and effects of deceased seamen (BT 153) are available for 1852-1881 and 1888-1889, with a name index in BT 154, and an index to Ships' Names (BT 155). There are also records of inquiries into Deaths at Sea, 1939-1964 (BT 341). Some earlier records of deceased merchant seamen's wages and effects (1798-1834) are in ADM 80/6-12 , but these are unindexed.

More information on records of deaths at sea can be found in a TNA research guide:

- Births, Marriages and Deaths at Sea
  www.nationalarchives.gov.uk/records/research-guides/
  births-marriages-deaths-sea.htm

The GRO holds registers of deaths compiled by overseas consuls since 1849, and also by the armed forces. The Marine Registers record deaths on board British merchant and naval vessels since 1837. There are registers of deaths that occurred in the Boer War and both World Wars. There are also registers of deaths on civil aircraft from 1948. For a detailed list of overseas registers in the GRO, see:

- General Register Events: Overseas Events Orders
  www.gro.gov.uk/gro/content/certificates/faqs-overseas.asp

A number of GRO collections relating to overseas deaths are now held in TNA. Many death certificates issued by foreign jurisdictions, copies of register entries made by English overseas clergy, and similar documents, can be found in RG 32. RG 33 includes both original registers and copies of entries from the registers of overseas churches and embassies. There are also some letters and miscellaneous memoranda. Many foreign death certificates can be found in RG 35, together with copies of entries in embassy registers etc. This class also includes a collection of certificates of British military deaths, 1914 to 1921, issued by the French and Belgian registration authorities. Notifications of deaths in some African and Asian colonial jurisdictions 1895-1965 are in RG 36. All of these classes are indexed in RG 43.

In addition, TNA holds a small number of regimental registers amongst its War Office (WO) collections. Much useful information on deaths at sea and overseas, together with lists of registers held by TNA, can be found in:

- BEVAN, AMANDA. *Tracing your ancestors in the National Archives: the website and beyond.* 7th ed. The National Archives, 2006.

Another major collection of overseas registers is held by the British Library. Chaplains of the East India Company kept registers of burials, and sent copies to their London head office. Entries generally relate to people of British descent - although one gives details of Napoleon's burial on St. Helena. The bulk of these registers come from the Indian sub-continent, but East India Company chaplains were stationed at many other places between the Atlantic and China. The registers record the name of the deceased, together with the date of death, age, occupation, the cause of death (after 1850), the date and place of burial, and the name of the officiating minister.

These transcripts are now held in the British Library's Oriental collections. They have been digitised and indexed, and can be searched at:
* India Office Family History Search
  http://indiafamily.bl.uk/UI

Further Reading
Only a very brief summary of the resources available for tracing overseas deaths and burials can be given here. Much more detail is provided in the following two books:
* *The British overseas: a guide to records of their births, baptisms, marriages, deaths and burials available in the United Kingdom.* 3rd ed. Guildhall Library, 1994.
* WATTS, CHRISTOPHER T., & WATTS, MICHAEL J. *Tracing births, deaths and marriages at sea.* Society of Genealogists Enterprises, 2004.

A more general guide to overseas research is provided by:
* KERSHAW, ROGER. *Emigrants and expats: a guide to sources on UK emigration and residents overseas.* Public Record Office, 2002.

13. Monumental Inscriptions

Registers are not the only source of information on deaths and burials. A variety of other sources are also available. Monumental inscriptions (frequently referred to as MIs) are amongst the most useful. They were known in the ancient world, and in the medieval period the aristocracy and gentry were frequently memorialised in stone or brass. In the eighteenth century the practice became more widespread. Churches, churchyards and cemeteries are now full of nineteenth and twentieth-century memorial stones, and it is highly likely that at least some of your ancestors have been remembered in this way.

There is no standard format for memorial inscriptions. Some simply give a name and a date. Others may provide detailed genealogical information for several generations of a family. Occupations, ages, and places of origin and residence may be mentioned. The deceased may be eulogised in verse. Scriptural quotations are common.

Locating memorials is not necessarily easy, given that GRO death certificates do not give the place of burial. If you have located an entry in a parish or cemetery register, that may help - especially the latter, since it may state the plot number of the grave. If you find one MI, then check nearby stones for memorials to other members of the family.

Family history societies and other researchers have compiled innumerable transcripts of MIs for particular places. It has been a common practice to make three copies of these transcripts, which are usually deposited with family history societies, the relevant local studies library or record office, and the Society of Genealogists **www.sog.org.uk**. The latter holds an enormous collection of transcripts. They can be searched by place in their on-line catalogue. Briefer details are given on their 'Geographical resources' pages (click 'library'). Lists of MI transcripts held can also sometimes be found on the webpages of local studies libraries and record offices.

Many family history societies have published MIs, both on fiche, and in hard copy. Their websites (listed at **www.genuki.org.uk/Societies**) usually include lists of their publications, and sometimes also have MI databases.

A substantial number of MI transcripts and indexes etc can be found on the internet. For some examples, see:

- Find A Grave
  www.findagrave.com
  International site
- Kent Archaeological Society: Churchyard Monumental Inscriptions
  www.kentarchaeology.org.uk/Research/Libr/MIs/MIslist.htm
- Norfolk Family History Society: Monumental Inscriptions Project
  www.norfolkfhs.org.uk/projects/monumentinscript.htm
- British Association for Cemeteries in South Asia
  www.bacsa.org.uk

14. War Memorials

Numerous war memorials can be found in town and village squares throughout the UK, and also abroad. They mainly commemorate men and women who died in the two world wars, although those killed in other conflicts may also be recorded. Frequently, they list all the men who died from a particular place, sometimes giving ranks, units, and other information. War memorials can also frequently be found in schools, railway stations, hospitals, police stations, churches, and a variety of other institutions. The most comprehensive listing of these memorials (although by no means exhaustive) is provided by:

- UK National Inventory of War Memorials
  www.ukniwm.org.uk

Many are also listed (with some photographs) at:
- Roll of Honour: Least We Forget
  www.roll-of-honour.com/Memorials

The graves of British servicemen who died in conflict are maintained by the Commonwealth War Graves Commission. Its database records the names of 1,700,000 men and women, with details of the 23,000 cemeteries and other places where they are commemorated. It includes details of rank, service number, date of death, age, regiment, nationality, grave/memorial reference, and Cemetery or memorial. Visit:

- Debt of Honour Register
  www.cwgc.org/debt_of_honour.asp

The names of servicemen who died in the First World War are listed in:
- *Officers died in the Great War, 1914-1919.* New ed. J.B. Hayward, c1988. Originally published HMSO, 1919
- *Soldiers died in the great war, 1914-19.* 80 pts in 6 vols. HMSO, 1920-1921. Reprinted J.B.Hayward, 1988.

Both these works are available on CD. An online database is also available at:
- Military-Genealogy.com
  www.military-genealogy.com
  This site includes a number of other databases.

There are numerous other war memorial sites on the internet, which cannot be listed here.

15. Coroners' Records

If one of your ancestors died unnaturally, in suspicious circumstances, or suddenly, the death should have been reported to the local coroner. Until 1926, he had to conduct all inquests with a jury. The results were frequently reported in local newspapers. If you are looking for details of an inquest, it is best to start by checking newspapers (see below, p. 20-21).

Many coroners records have been lost. Nevertheless, much survives, and it is worth finding out what is available. Records can be found in both local record offices, and in TNA. Originally, a coroner handed his papers to the judges of the Eyre courts, or (later) of Assizes, who took them to file with their records. These are now in various classes in TNA. From 1752 until 1860, coroners' records were kept with Quarter Sessions records, which are in local record offces. Records after 1860 were retained by coroners, but many can now be found in local record offices. In the few cases where a coroner's inquest resulted in a trial for murder or manslaughter, details will be held with the trial papers in TNA.

A variety of documents are available. Local record offices may have inquests, which summarise hearings, and give verdicts . They also give details of the deceased, the date of death, and the names of jurors. Coroners' registers record the deaths brought to their attention, giving names and addresses of the deceased, and dates and places of death. Coroners' bills, frequently found amongst Quarter

Sessions records, commence in 1752, and record the expenses incurred by the coroner for each inquest. The information provided includes the name of the deceased, the date and place of the inquest, details of the expenses claimed, and sometimes the verdict.

Earlier coroners' records, found in TNA, are written in Latin, and may be difficult to use (although some have been published). Between 1487 and 1752, records were stored with the indictment files of Kings Bench (class KB 9 and KB 11). Most earlier records are in JUST 2, although a variety of other classes hold related papers. These are too specialised to consider here.

Further Reading
For a brief introduction to the records, consult:
* 'Coroners' inquests', in BEVAN, AMANDA. *Tracing your ancestors in the National Archives.* 7th ed. National Archives, 2006 p.422-5.

See also:
* Coroners' Inquests
  **www.nationalarchives.gov.uk/records/research-guides/
  coroners-inquests.htm**

A comprehensive listing of all surviving coroners records, which includes details of relevant publications, is provided by:
* GIBSON, JEREMY, & ROGERS, COLIN. *Coroners records in England and Wales.* 3rd ed. Family History Partnership, 2009.

Many individual inquests and other records in TNA can be identified in its online catalogue. Calendars of some coroners records held by local record offices can sometimes be found on their websites, and also at:
* A2A: Access to Archives
  www.nationalarchives.gov/a2a

16. Wills & other Probate Records
Wills are the most personal documents relating to your ancestors that you are likely to encounter. They contain their instructions for the disposal of their assets. They should include their signatures, or at least their marks. Sometimes they are in their own hand. Other probate documents may also be useful. Probate inventories list ancestors' possessions. Accounts describe how their assets were distributed. Administration bonds name administrators and sometimes other relatives. Wills do not give dates of death, but they were frequently written when the testator was at death's door, and are likely to give the date on which probate was granted.

Wills contain invaluable genealogical information. They usually identify parishes of residence, and sometimes the actual house. Most testators mention their widows and all their surviving children in their wills. Choice of an executor was usually made from members of the immediate family. Other relatives may also be mentioned. Landed property - especially leasehold - held by the deceased was sometimes mentioned in either the will or the inventory. Wills may also reveal interesting personal information. Testators may have been protective towards their widows, dismissive of wayward children, and appreciative of the work of a servant. If you can find a will written by an ancestor, it may shed much light on the history of your family.

Until 1857, most wills were proved in ecclesiastical courts. Their records are usually to be found in local record offices, although the records of the major probate court - the Prerogative Court of Canterbury - are now in TNA. A detailed guide to probate courts and the availability of wills is provided by:
- GIBSON, JEREMY, & CHURCHILL, ELSE. *Probate jurisdictions: where to look for wills.* 5th ed. F.F.H.S, 2002. This includes details of many published indexes to wills. New edition from the Family History Partnership forthcoming.

Over 1,000,000 wills have been digitised on TNA's Documents Online site:
- The National Archives: Documents Online: Prerogative Court of Canterbury wills (1384-1858)
  www.nationalarchives.gov.uk/documentsonline/wills.asp

For another major collection of digitised wills, visit:
- Wiltshire Wills
  www.wshc.eu/about-wshc/archives/209.html

Welsh wills have been digitised at
- National Library of Wales: Wills and Probate Records
  http://www.llgc.org.uk/index.php?id=487

A variety of indexes to wills are available on the internet. These are listed in:
- RAYMOND, STUART A. *Family history on the web: a directory for England and Wales.* 5th ed. Family History Partnership, 2008.

In 1858, the ecclesiastical probate courts were abolished. Since then, wills have been proved in the Court of Probate, and filed in the Probate Registry. Details of the procedure for consultation, are given on the Court's page:
- Probate Records and Family History
  www.justice.gov.uk/guidance/courts-and-tribunals/courts/probate/family-history.htm

Further Reading
It is not possible here to provide more than a brief summary of information regarding probate records. A basic introduction is provided by:
- Wills and Probate Records
  www.nationalarchives.gov.uk/records/research-guides/wills-and-probate-records.htm

A detailed and extensive introduction to probate records is provided by:
- GRANNUM, KAREN, & TAYLOR, NIGEL. *Wills & probate records: a guide for family historians.* 2nd ed. TNA, 2009.

17. Death Duties

The records of death duties are closely related to probate records. The term actually encompasses the legacy duty (from 1796), succession duty (from 1853), and estate duty (from 1894). Registers were kept from 1796 until 1903. Some of the information in these registers was taken from probate records, and the indexes in IR 27 can be used to identify the court in which a will was proved.

Death duty registers, dating from 1796 to 1903, are held by TNA, in class IR 26. These registers include information not found elsewhere. They provide much interesting information concerning both the deceased, his next of kin, and his legatees. They could be annotated for many years after the date of death, so may give information about the deaths of widows and legatees, and the births of descendants.

Early registers have been digitised, and can be searched online at:
- Death Duty Registers (1796-1811)
  www.nationalarchives.gov.uk/documentsonline/death-duty.asp

Some registers have been microfilmed for the LDS. Details are given in their library catalogue at **www.familysearch.org** (Click 'catalog')

Further Reading
- Death Duty Registers 1796 to 1903
  www.nationalarchives.gov.uk/records/research-guides/ death-duty-records-1796-to-1903.htm

18. Church Records

Wills can occasionally also be found amongst the records of charities formerly kept in parish chests. Many charities were founded by wills, and charity records can occasionally provide useful information about benefactors. Parish benefactors are also frequently recorded on boards in churches. When you are visiting a church looking for monumental inscriptions, look out for these boards as well.

A variety of other church records may also provide information on deaths and burials. Parish registers have already been discussed. The medieval belief in purgatory, and in the value of prayers for the dead, created numerous records. Unfortunately, most were destroyed during the Reformation. However, those which survive may well be useful if you are tracing pre-Reformation ancestors.

A variety of obit accounts survive amongst cathedral archives and elsewhere. These record payments made to priests who said regular masses for the deceased, naming the latter. Those for Exeter are printed in:

- LEPINE, DAVID, & ORME, NICHOLAS, eds. *Death and memory in medieval Exeter.* Devon & Cornwall Record Society, new series **47**. 2003.

Bede rolls listed deceased parishioners who had contributed to church funds, and therefore had to be prayed for. These lists were regularly read out from the pulpit. Sadly, most were lost during the Reformation. Sometimes, however, related evidence can be found in churchwardens' accounts, as at Morebath in Devon. There, the vicar in 1540 listed in the accounts all the benefactions to the parish which had been made in the previous twenty years. Pre-Reformation accounts may also record payment for lights, i.e. candles, used at funerals, naming the deceased.

Some things were not changed by the Reformation. Bequests made by parishioners, payments made for burial inside churches, and fees paid for ringing the knells at funerals, may all be recorded in churchwardens accounts. All of these entries may enable you to date the death and/or burial of an ancestor. For a useful introduction to churchwardens' accounts, provided by the Borthwick Institute of Historical Research, see:

- Churchwardens Accounts
  www.york.ac.uk/media/library/documents/borthwick/ 5Churchwardenabt.pdf

See also:
- Cox, J.C. *Churchwardens' accounts from the fourteenth century to the close of the seventeenth century.* Methuen, 1913.

Overseers accounts may also provide useful information. The office of parish overseer was created by the Elizabethan poor law statutes of 1598 and 1601. They had the duty of relieving the poor – a task which included the duty of paying for the burials of paupers. Expenses, eg for coffins, are recorded in overseers' accounts.

A useful perquisite for many clergymen was the mortuary that was due to the incumbent on the death of a parishioner. Occasionally, the receipt of these fees was recorded, and accounts of receipts may usefully list the parish dead. These accounts may be found amongst parish records.

Parish records have usually been deposited in local record offices, whose catalogues should be consulted. They may also be searched for at A2A: Access to Archives **www.nationalarchives.gov.uk/a2a**

19. Funeral Certificates

Funeral certificates were compiled by the Heralds of the College of Arms **http://college-of-arms.gov.uk** when they organized funerals of the nobility and gentry, between the sixteenth and the eighteenth centuries. In addition to heraldic information, certificates include details of the death, burial, and family of the deceased. Some are held by the College of Arms, which is unfortunately closed to most researchers; others can be found in the British Library. Two collections have been published:

- RYLANDS, JOHN PAUL, ed. *Cheshire and Lancashire funeral certificates,* A.D.1600 to 1678. Lancashire and Cheshire Record Society, **6**. 1882.
- KING, THOMAS WILLIAM, ed. *Lancashire funeral certificates.* Chetham Society old series, **75**. 1869.

20. Newspapers & Journals

Death notices in newspapers are an invaluable source of information, and became common in the nineteenth century. Many newspapers also carried obituaries and accounts of funerals, and sometimes coroners' inquests were reported. If you know a date of death, it is worth checking local newspapers to see if your ancestor was mentioned. They are usually available in the relevant local studies library, as well as in the British Library. For a detailed list of local newspapers, with locations, consult:

- GIBSON, JEREMY, LANGSTON, BRETT, & SMITH, BRENDA W. *Local newspapers 1750-1920: England and Wales, Channel Islands, Isle of Man: a select location list.* 3rd ed. Family History Partnership, 2011.

Most historic newspapers are available for consultation in the
- British Library Newspaper Reading Room
  www.bl.uk/reshelp/inrrooms/blnewspapers/newsrr.html

Until recently, it was difficult to check newspapers if you did not have a date of death. However, an increasing number are now being digitised, and are becoming available online. They can be searched at the click of a button. 2,000,000 pages from 49 newspapers are currently available at
- British Newspapers 1800-1900
  http://newspapers.bl.uk/blcs

If your ancestors were prominent people, death notices or obituaries may have been placed in the Times. Its index is widely available in libraries, as is microfilm of its text. It is also available online. The website requires payment of a subscription, but it is frequently freely available through public library sites:
- Times Online
  http://archive.timesonline.co.uk/tol/archive

Times obituaries are also available in printed books:
• ROBERTS, F.C., ed. *Obituaries from the Times 1951-60.* 1979. Further volumes cover 1961-70 and 1971-75.

Obituaries and death notices in the Guardian, the Observer, and the Scotsman, can all be searched online. Visit:
• The Guardian / The Observer Digital Archive
http://archive.guardian.co.uk
• The Scotsman Digital Archive
http://archive.scotsman.com

The British Library's Newspaper Library also holds numerous journals and magazines which carried obituaries. Many obituaries of churchmen, for example, can be found in the the journals of the various denominations. Trade and professional journals carried many obituaries of people engaged in particular occupations. County historical journals frequently have obituaries of local historians and, indeed, genealogists. If you know that your ancestor was active in a particular field, then identify the journals which were devoted to that activity, and check them for obituaries.

Many older obituaries are indexed in:
• MUSGRAVE, W., SIR. *Obituary prior to 1800 as far as relates to England, Scotland and Ireland.* 6 vols. Harleian Society, **44-9**. 1899-1901.

The Gentleman's magazine, which is widely available in libraries, carried many obituaries of the middle and upper classes. These are indexed in:
• NANGLE, B. *The Gentleman's Magazine biographical and obituary notices, 1781-1819: an index.* Garland, 1980.

Further Reading
• CHAPMAN, COLIN R. *Using newspapers and periodicals.* FFHS, 1993.
• MURPHY, MICHAEL. *Newspapers and local history.* Phillimore, for the British Association for Local History, 1991.

21. Manorial Records
For most of the last millenium, land in England was usually held of a manorial lord. It was not until 1922 that the last vestiges of the manorial system were abolished. If your ancestors rented property, then their tenancies would have been recorded in manorial records. Manors were governed through manorial courts.
    A wide range of business is recorded in early court rolls. The subjects dealt with are normally clearly separated in them, but the only topic which directly concerns us here are the records of surrenders and admissions. Tenants who had died are identified in these records. Dates of death, details of the property held, and the names of heirs, are all given. In a parish where all the land was controlled

by the manor court, and tenanted, the court roll should provide information relating to a large proportion of adult males - and some females - who died. All tenants should be recorded. Their heirs are likely to be named. Court rolls are therefore likely to be a valuable aid to the family historians, especially if parish registers are missing.

As the eighteenth and nineteenth centuries progressed, business in manorial courts became confined to the admissions and surrenders of copyhold tenants. Manorial courts gradually ceased to meet, although changes of tenants continued to be recorded in court books. The Law of Property Act 1922 abolished copyhold tenancies, and manorial records ceased.

Before the mid-eighteenth century, many manorial records are in Latin. However, much of the language used is common form, continuously repeated. Reading it may require some persistence, but is not impossible. A useful manual to help you read Latin documents is provided by:

* STUART, D. *Manorial records: an introduction to their transcription and translation.* Phillimore, 1992.

Manorial court records can be found in most record offices, national and local. Local record offices frequently hold records from outside of their own area, since manors were frequently owned by estates which had properties in several counties, and all the estate records are kept together. Locations can be identified in the Manorial Documents Register **www.nationalarchives.gov.uk/mdr**. For a useful introduction to the register, consult:

* The Manorial Documents Register and Manorial Lordships
  **www.nationalarchives.gov.uk/records/research-guides/
  manorial-documents-register-lordships.htm**

Further Reading
Useful advice pages on the internet include:
* Manor and other Local Court Rolls, 13th century to 1922
  **www.nationalarchives.gov.uk/records/research-guides/
  manor-court-rolls.htm**
* Manorial Records
  **www.nationalarchives.gov.uk/records/research-guides/
  manorial-records.htm**
* Cumbrian Manorial Records
  www.lancs.ac.uk/fass/projects/manorialrecords/index.htm

More extensive guidance is provided by:
* ELLIS, MARY. *Using manorial records.* 2nd ed. Readers guide 6. Public Record Office, 1997.
* HARVEY, P.D.A. *Manorial records.* Rev. ed. Archives and the user 5. British Records Association, 1999
* PARK, PETER B. *My ancestors were manorial tenants.* Society of Genealogists Enterprises, 2005.

22. Inquisitions Post Mortem

In feudal law, the death of a tenant in chief entitled the Crown to receive a relief from the heir. If the heir was under age, the Crown was entitled to the revenue from the estate, and could select the heir's bride. These rights were sold to the highest bidder.

The extent of the crown's rights were determined by a local jury, who provided the information which the Crown's escheator needed in order to compile an inquisition post mortem (IPM). These give details of lands held, date of death, and the name and age of the heir. They run from 1235 until 1646.

IPMs are now held by TNA, amongst the records of the Court of Chancery (C132), the Court of Exchequer (E149), and the Court of Wards and Liveries (WARD7). They are written in Latin. Comprehensive calendars for the dates mentioned are published in:

- *Calendar of inquisitions post mortem and other analogous documents preserved in the Public Record Office.* HMSO (continued by Boydell & Brewer),1904-. To be continued. lst series (26 vols.) covers 1235-1447; 2nd series (3 vols.) covers 1485-1509.

Some of these calendars, together with others for particular county, have been digitised. For details, see:
- Medieval source material on the internet: Inquisitions post mortem **www.medievalgenealogy.org.uk/sources/ipm.shtml**

An index to uncalendared IPMs is provided by:
- *Index of inquisitions preserved in the Public Record Office.* Lists & indexes **23, 26, 31, & 33.** Amended ed. New York: Kraus Reprint, 1963. Contents: v.1. Henry VIII to Philip & Mary. v.2. Elizabeth. v.3. James I. v.4. Charles I and later.

Further Reading
- Inquisitions post mortem, Henry III - Charles I: landholders and heirs **www.nationalarchives.gov.uk/records/research-guides/inqusitions-post-mortem.htm90**
- MC GUINNESS, MARY. 'Inquisitions post mortem', in STEEL, D. J. *Sources of births, marriages and deaths before 1837 (I).* National index of parish registers **1**. Society of Genealogists, 1968, p.367-71.

23. Channel Isles

Each of the Channel Islands had their own system of civil registration. Death registration began in the following years: Alderney 1850; Guernsey 1840; Jersey 1842; Sark 1915.

Addresses for the registrars are given below p.39. A fiche index to Jersey death registers for 1842-1900 is held by the Channel Islands Family History Society www.jerseyfamilyhistory.org, and by the Société Jersiase www.societe-jersiaise.org. For Guernsey, copies of the actual registers are held by the Society of Genealogists (for 1840-1907) and the Priaulx Library www.priaulxlibrary.co.uk (19th c.). The Society of Genealogists also has an index extending to 1963.

Channel Island parish registers are frequently still held by churches. There are no bishops' transcripts. For Jersey, some original registers are held at the Jersey Archive www.jerseyheritage.org/research-centre/jersey-archive. Most pre-1842 registers have been transcribed by the Channel Islands Family History Society. The Priaulx Library holds a few original Guernsey registers, plus copies of most of the others. The Society of Genealogists holds a few copies of Channel Island registers.

Full details of both civil and parish registers are given in:
* WEBB, CLIFF. *National index of parish registers ... Channel Islands and the Isle of Man*. Society of Genealogists, 2000.

It may also be useful to visit:
* Alex Glendinning's Channel Islands Pages
  http://user.itl.net/~glen/CIintro.html

24. Ireland

24A. Irish Civil Registration
The civil registration of deaths in Ireland commenced in 1864. Since 1st July 1922, vital events have been registered separately in Northern Ireland. Death certificates include the date and place of death, the name of the deceased, sex, marital status, age (sometimes approximate), occupation, and the cause of death (with the duration of the final illness). The informant (who was not necessarily a relative), and the registrar, were required to sign and date each entry in the register. The informant's residence and qualification for reporting the death were also stated.

Indexes to the civil registers have been computerised, but are not available online. Details of GRO register entries can be obtained from the appropriate GRO in Dublin or Belfast. In Dublin, it is possible to obtain either a photocopy of the original register, or a certificate. For genealogical purposes, the former is preferable, since it avoids any error in copying. It is also cheaper. For post-1924 deaths, you can request certificates which incorporate a photographic image of the original entry. In Belfast, certificates only are available. It is also possible to obtain death certificates from district registrars.

The websites of the two General Register Offices (which include lists of district registrars) are as follows:
* General Register Office [Eire]
  www.groireland.ie
* General Register Office (GRO) Information
  www.groni.gov.uk
  For Northern Ireland

District registrars are also listed by
- Superintendent Registrars' Districts by County
  www.rootsweb.ancestry.com/~bifhsusa/irishregnc.html

Copies of most civil registration death indexes for 1864-1958 (1959 for Northern Ireland) are held by the LDS Family History Library, and are available through its network of Family History Centers. They are also available online:
- Ireland Civil Registration Indexes
  https://wiki.familysearch.org/en/Ireland,_Civil_Registration_Indexes_(FamilySearch_Historical_Records)

The LDS also holds copies of the actual death registers for 1864-70 (all Ireland), and for 1922-59 (Northern Ireland). Certificates can also be obtained from district registrars, some of whom will allow you to personally consult their registers. Indexes to a few of their death registers have been compiled by Irish Family History Foundation centres **www.irish-roots.ie**. If you know places of death, it is better to obtain death certificates from district registrars, since they hold the original registers. The Irish GRO registers are copies of them, and are therefore open to the errors possible during the copying process.

Irish GRO indexes up to 1877 were annual; thereafter they were quarterly. They include the basic information needed to order certificates, that is, the name, the Registration District, and the volume and page number in which the entry is recorded. Indexes to the registers of district registrars cannot be used to identify entries in the Irish GRO registerst. The volume and page numbers given differ.

More information is provided by a number of webpages:
- Civil Registration
  http//freepages.genealogy.rootsweb.ancestry.com/~irishancestors/Civil%20registration.html
- Family Search Research Wiki; Ireland Civil Registration
  https://wiki.familysearch.org/en/Ireland_Civil_Registration
- A Guide to the General Register Office of Ireland
  http://homepage.eircom.net/~seanjmurphy/gro

24B. Irish Ecclesiastical Registration
Many death and burial registers compiled by the clergy of various denominations are available. For a useful introduction, consult:
- Family Search: Ireland Church Records
  https://wiki.familysearch.org/en/Ireland_Church_Records

The Roman Catholic Church has always been the dominant denomination in Ireland, despite the fact that the Church of Ireland was the established church. It is likely that the Irish researcher will need to consult Roman Catholic parish registers. Sadly, many Church of Ireland parish registers were destroyed by fire in 1922, together with most bishops' transcripts. Bear in mind that Roman Catholic and Church of Ireland parishes do not necessarily have the same boundaries or the same names.

A number of other denominations can be found in Ireland. Presbyterians were particularly important (especially in Northern Ireland), but there were also Quakers, Baptists, Methodists, and others, many of whom kept registers.

Over the centuries there have been many upheavals in Ireland, which have not been conducive to good record keeping. Few registers of any denomination pre-date the eighteenth century, and most commence much later.

Many registers have been microfilmed and deposited in both the National Library of Ireland (especially Roman Catholic registers), and the Public Record of Northern Ireland. For these, see:

- National Library of Ireland: Parish Registers
  www.nli.ie/en/parish-register.aspx
- Your Family Tree series 3: Church Records
  www.proni.gov.uk/your_family_tree_series_-_03_-_church_records.pdf

A few original registers and microfilms are also held in the National Archives of Ireland. Visit:

- The National Archives of Ireland: Parish Records and Marriage Licences
  www.nationalarchives.ie/genealogy/church.html

Original Roman Catholic registers are mostly still in church custody. For a comprehensive listing of register transcripts and indexes, see:

- Irish Ancestors: Roman Catholic records
  www.irishtimes.com/ancestor/browse/counties/rcmaps

Most surviving Church of Ireland registers for the Irish Republic are now deposited in the Representative Church Body Library **www.library.ireland.anglican.org**, which has published a number of them.

Many Presbyterian registers are still in local custody. Some have been deposited with the:

- Presbyterian Historical Society of Ireland
  www.presbyterianhistoryireland.com/index.php?id=library

Most Methodist registers are still held by churches. Many from Northern Ireland have been microfilmed by the Public Record Office of Northern Ireland (see above). They have also filmed many Quaker registers. Original Quaker registers are held in:

- Quakers in Ireland: Historical Library
  http://www.quakers-in-ireland.ie/historical-library

Further Reading
A comprehensive guide to Irish ecclesiastical registers is provided by:
* RYAN, JAMES G., ed. *Irish Church Records.* Glenageary, County Dublin, Ireland: Flyleaf Press, 1992.

Comprehensive lists of registers are also included in:
* GREENHAM, JOHN. *Tracing your Irish ancestors: the complete guide.* 3rd ed. Gill & Macmillan, 2006.

Numerous webpages are devoted to Irish death registers. These are listed in:
* RAYMOND, STUART A. *Irish family history on the web: a directory.* 3rd ed. Family History Partnership, 2007.

25. Isle of Man
In the Isle of Man, civil registration of deaths commenced in 1884. The registers are open to public inspection. The address of the Civil Registry is given below, p.39. Microfilmed copies of the indexes are held by the Society of Genealogists up to 1964.

Parish registers are similar in form to English registers, and some date from the seventeenth century. From 1849, transcripts had to be made annually; these are now held by the Civil Registry. In 1910, all registers prior to 1849 were copied. These copies, together with original registers 1849-83, have been microfilmed and are available for consultation in the Manx Museum **www.gov.im/lib/docs/ mnh/heritage/library/publicinformationsheet1.pdf.**

Many pre-1797 monumental inscriptions are published in:
* FELTHAM, JOHN, & WRIGHT, EDWARD, ed. *Memorials of "God's Acre": being monumental inscriptions in the Isle of Man, taken in the summer of 1797,* ed. William Harrison. Douglas: Manx Society, 1868.

The burial registers, and many monumental inscriptions, have been transcribed and published by the Isle of Man Family History Society. Visit:
* Isle of Man Family History Society Publications List **www.isleofman.com/heritage/genealogy/fhs/publications.aspx**

An index to the burial registers is available for online searching:
* Burials: Main Index and Notes **www.iomfhs.im/lawsons/LawsonBMD/burials/_bur_index.html?Submit= Burials**

Full details of both civil and parish registers are given in:
* WEBB, CLIFF. *National index of parish registers ... Channel Islands and the Isle of Man.* Society of Genealogists, 2000.

Some extracts from burial registers, with much other useful information, is provided by:
* A Manx Notebook: an electronic compendium of matters past and present connected with the Isle of Man / Francis Coakley (ed.)
  www.isle-of-man.com/manxnotebook

26. Scotland
Scottish civil registers, old parish registers, and Roman Catholic registers, can all be found on one website:
* Scotlands People
  www.scotlandspeople.gov.uk

Various other sources of information on deaths and burials are also available. For a useful introduction, visit:
* Scottish Archives Network. Knowledge Base: Records of Death and Burial
  www.scan.org.uk/knowledgebase/topics/deathandburial_topic.htm

26A. Civil Registration
Civil registration in Scotland began on 1st January 1855. Burial registers for 1855-9 include columns for:
* 'name, rank, profession or occupation'
* sex
* age
* 'where born, and how long in this district'
* 'parents names, and rank profession or occupation'
* 'if deceased was married', and, if so, 'to whom', together with 'issue in order of birth, their names and ages',
* 'when died, year, day of month, hour'
* 'where died'
* 'cause of death, and how long disease continued, medical attendant by whom certified, and when he last saw deceased',
* 'burial place; undertaker by whom certified',
* 'signature of informant'
* 'when and where registered, and signature of registrar'

Some of these columns were subsequently dropped. From 1856, the birthplace, and the names of children, were no longer required. Nor was the name of the spouse, although this was reinstated from 1861. From 1860, the place of burial, the name of the undertaker, and the time when the doctor last saw the deceased ceased to be required
  At the time of writing, an index of deaths is available for the period 1855-2006 on Scotlands People. Digitisation of the actual registers extends from 1855 to 1960.

This website also has digitised images up to 1960 of a number of minor records relating to Scottish residents. These include:

- the Air Register (from 1948) of deaths on British-registered aircraft.
- Consular Returns (from 1914).
- Foreign Returns (1860-1965) registering deaths abroad reported by interested parties.
- High Commission Returns (from 1964) of deaths in certain Commonwealth countries.
- Marine Register (from 1855) of deaths at sea (including deaths of service personnel).
- Service Returns (from 1881) of deaths at military stations abroad.
- War Returns, include registers of deaths of Scottish soldiers in the South African War (1899-1902), and some army and naval personnel in World Wars I & II.

A personal visit to consult the records is also possible. Scotlands People Centre **www.scotlandspeoplehub.gov.uk** has computerized indexes to all civil registers, to the old parish registers, and to a variety of overseas registers. If you are not able to visit, then application can be made for certificates direct to:

- General Register Office for Scotland
  www.gro-scotland.gov.uk

An alternative source of information is provided by the LDS Family History Library. They hold microfilmed copies of Scottish death registers 1855-75, 1881, and 1891. They also hold indexes, 1855-1956. For full details, consult:

- Family Search: Scotland Civil Registration: Vital Records
  https://wiki.familysearch.org/en/Scotland_Civil_Registration-_Vital_Records

The Society of Genealogists has a microfilmed copy of the original deaths register, but only for 1855. It also has the microfilmed death indexes for 1855-1920.

26B. Old Parish Registers, Ecclesiastical Registers, & Cemetery Registers
The (Presbyterian) Church of Scotland was the established church in Scotland. Its registers sometimes included entries relating to death or burial. There was no set format for these, no equivalent to English bishops' transcripts, and, disappointingly, no requirement for entries to be made at all. Consequently, death registration in the old parish registers is very poor, and many have disappeared (if they were ever kept). All the registers that were in existence when civil registration was introduced in 1855 were called in by the Scottish Registrar General. They have been digitised and indexed by Scotlands People. The earliest commences in 1553, but most are much later. This collection closes in 1854.

Microfilm copies of the old parish registers are frequently to be found in local libraries and record offices. Sometimes, more recent burial registers (including cemetery registers) are held by them as well. For a union catalogue of Scottish archives, together with a record office directory, visit:

* The Scottish Archive Network
  www.scan.org.uk

The Network's catalogue can also be used to locate registers from other denominations. A variety of denominations were active in Scotland, and kept burial registers. The National Archives of Scotland **www.nas.gov.uk** hold some original registers from the Episcopal Church, and also some microfilms. Quakers, Methodists, and Congregationalists were also active in Scotland. Some of their registers are held locally, some have been deposited with the National Archives of Scotland. The National Archives also holds some Roman Catholic registers. Others have been deposited in the:

* Scottish Catholic Archive
  www.scottishcatholicarchives.org.uk

The birth and baptism entries from Roman Catholic registers have been digitised by Scotlands People. It is to be hoped that burial entries will follow.

An increasing number of Scottish cemetery registers and monumental inscriptions can be searched at:

* Deceased Online
  www.deceasedonline.com

Further Reading
The authoritative guide to Scottish registers is:

* Steel, D.J., & Steel, A.A.E. *Sources for Scottish genealogy and family history.* National index of parish registers **12**. Society of Genealogists, 1970.

For Scottish burial registers and monumental inscriptions on the internet, consult:

* Raymond, Stuart A. *Scottish family history on the web: a directory.* 3rd ed. Family History Partnership, 2010.

27. Clues in other Sources
There are many other sources that may help you trace your ancestor's death, burial, and grave. For example, the cessation of regular entries in the census, in trade directories, or in electoral registers, may suggest that a death has taken place. Estate rentals and surveys may record changes of tenancy, from which it may be possible to infer a death. Family bibles may record deaths of family members. You may find funeral cards and programmes amongst family papers. Criminal records may provide information about individuals who have been murdered.

There is more to tracing family history than just pressing a few buttons on the internet. If you are serious about tracing your ancestors, you will want to identify every source that mentions them. That will help you to build up as detailed a picture of their lives as is possible.

If this is what you want to do, then you will need to explore the resources offered by libraries and record offices. You will need to join a family history society. And you will need to consult manuals which explain what sources are available, where you can find them, and how to use them. For a basic introduction, consult:

- RAYMOND, STUART A. *Introducing family history*. FFHS, 2006.

The most comprehensive manual is:

- HERBER, MARK. *Ancestral trails*. Sutton, 2004.

28. Useful Addresses

A. General Register Offices

Channel Islands
Alderney: The Greffier, Registry for Births, Deaths, Companies, Land and
    Marriages, St Anne, Alderney, GY9 3AA
Guernsey: H.M. Greffier, The Royal Court House, St Peter Port, Guernsey,
    GY1 2PB
Jersey: The Superintendent Registrar, 10 Royal Square, St. Helier, Jersey, JE2 4WA
Sark: The Greffe, La Chasse Marette, Sark, GY9 0SF

England
General Register Office, PO Box 2 , Southport, PR8 2JD
    www.gro.gov.uk/gro/content

Ireland
General Register Office, Government Offices, Convent Road, Roscommon, Eire
    www.groireland.ie

Isle of Man
Douglas Civil Registry Office, Deemsters Walk, Douglas, Isle of Man, IM1 3AR
    www.gov.im/registries/general/civilregistry/welcome.xml

Northern Ireland
The General Register Office, Oxford House, 49-55 Chichester Street, Belfast,
    BT1 4HL
    www.nidirect.gov.uk/gro

Scotland
General Register Office for Scotland, New Register House, 3 West Register Street,
    Edinburgh,Scotland, EH1 3YT
    www.gro-scotland.gov.uk

B. Other Institutions: England

Guildhall Library, Aldermanbury, London, EC2V 7HH.
www.cityoflondon.gov.uk/Corporation/LGNL_Services/Leisure_and_culture/Libraries/City_of_London_libraries/guildhall_lib.htm

Institute of Heraldic & Genealogical Studies, 79-82 Northgate, Canterbury, Kent, CT1 1BA.
www.ihgs.ac.uk

Society of Genealogists, 14 Charterhouse Buildings, Goswell Road, London, EC1M 7BA.
www.sog.org.uk

The National Archives, Kew, Richmond, Surrey, TW9 4DU.
www.nationalarchives.gov.uk

The Library, Religious Society of Friends, Friends House, 173 - 177 Euston Road, London, NW1 2BJ.
www.quaker.org.uk/category/tags/library-religious-society-friends

C. Other Institutions: Ireland

The National Archives, Bishop Street, Dublin 8, Ireland.
www.nationalarchives.ie

Public Record Office of Northern Ireland, 2 Titanic Boulevard, Titanic Quarter, Belfast, BT3 9HQ.
www.proni.gov.uk

D. Other Institutions: Scotland

The National Archives of Scotland, H M General Register House, 2 Princes Street, Edinburgh, EH1 3YY
www.nas.gov.uk

The Scottish Genealogy Society, 15 Victoria Terrace, Edinburgh, EH1 2JL, Scotland
www.scotsgenealogy.com

Scotlands People Centre, HM General Register House, 2 Princes Street, Edinburgh, EH1 3YY
www.scotlandspeoplehub.gov.uk